THE BABY IN THE BASKET

Jennifer Rees Larcombe

Illustrated by Steve Björkman

Marshall Pickering
An Imprint of HarperCollins*Publishers*

Marshall Pickering is an Imprint of
HarperCollins*Religious*
Part of HarperCollins*Publishers*
77–85 Fulham Palace Road
London W6 8JB

First published in 1992 in Great Britain
by Marshall Pickering as part of
Children's Bible Story Book by Jennifer Rees Larcombe
This edition published in 1997 by Marshall Pickering

1 3 5 7 9 10 8 6 4 2

A catalogue record for this book is
available from the British Library

0 551 031182

Printed and bound in Italy by New Interlitho Italia S.P.A.

THE BABY IN THE BASKET

'Who **are** all those people?' stormed Pharaoh

the King of Egypt as his boat floated down the

River Nile. 'They're not

Egyptians!'

'No your Majesty,' replied his Chamberlain,

'they are Jews.' The Jews were God's very

own people, and they had been living in Egypt for hundreds of years.

'I don't like them!' said Pharaoh angrily.

'There are far too many of them, and they're living on the best land in my Kingdom. Just look at all their **fat sheep** eating my grass!'

I'll have to get rid of them. They might fight against us Egyptians one day, and anyway I want to use their land for building.'

'You shall be our

slaves!'

he shouted angrily
across the water.
'You'll work so hard
you'll

soon die.'

Day after day, in the blistering sun, the poor Jews were bullied by Egyptians with great whips. They hardly had any food as they were forced to build cities, palaces and pyramids.

'There are **still** too many of them,' muttered Pharaoh. **'Soldiers,'** he ordered, 'every time a Jewish baby boy is born, throw it into the river!'

'Oh God, help us!' cried the poor Jews, and

God heard them.

One day in a little slave hut, a very special baby
was born.

'We can't let him be drowned,' sobbed

his mother, 'but if we keep him here the soldiers
are bound to hear him cry.'

So they made a floating cradle for Moses, out of a waterproof basket. In the morning, long before anyone was awake, they crept down to the river and hid the basket amongst the reeds. Miriam, the baby's big sister, was left on guard.

The gentle lapping of the water soon rocked Moses to sleep, and Miriam began to weave a mat of reeds.

Then, suddenly, she was **stiff with fear.**

Someone was coming.

Down the path from the palace came the Princess, Pharaoh's own daughter. Poor Miriam was shaking with fright as she watched the Princess slide into the water for a swim.

'Wade over and get me that funny little basket,' said the Princess to one of her maids, and Miriam closed her eyes in horror.

'Oh look!' exclaimed the Princess.

'It's a darling little Jewish baby. I won't let father

drown him; he shall be mine for always.'

Just at that moment Moses began to cry loudly.

'Oh dear!' said the Princess

doubtfully. 'He's probably hungry.'

Quickly Miriam slipped out of her hiding place and said, 'Would you like me to find someone to look after your baby for you?'

'Thank you,' said the Princess. She was pleased to find someone to feed the baby.

Of course Miriam ran straight to fetch her mother, who looked after Moses as he grew up in the royal palace.

She told him the secret about the beautiful land God had promised to give his family one day.

'You must grow up to be a clever and powerful Prince, my son,' she would whisper.

'Then perhaps you can save your people from being slaves and take them back to their own land.'

Exodus 1; 2:2–10